Oceans A-

Contents

Humans and oceans   2
Oceans in motion   6
Life beneath the waves   9
Living communities   18
Oceans under threat   22
Working with the ocean   32
New discoveries   38
How can we help?   41
Glossary   44
Index   45
Save our oceans!   46

Written by Angie Belcher
Photographed by Andy Belcher

Collins

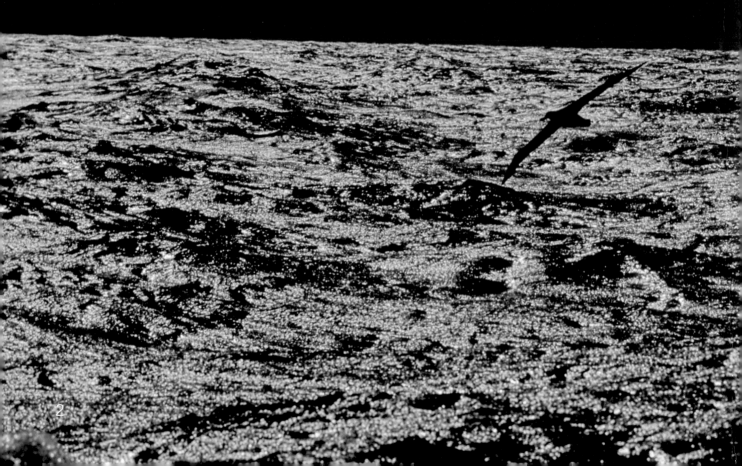

Have you ever looked out to sea and wondered what lives within it?
Or how important it is to us, even if we live many miles inland?

We need the sea. It gives us life. It gives us much of the oxygen we breathe and provides us with food and minerals. It provides the water that forms rain, filling our rivers, lakes and reservoirs.

We use it to transport people and cargo.
We play on it.

We use salt in our food.

Magnesium is used in rockets.

Gas and oil are found under the ocean floor.

There are five great oceans on Earth: the Pacific, Atlantic, Indian, Southern and Arctic Oceans. They hold 97% of all the water in the world and cover nearly 71% of the Earth's surface. Some oceans are warm, others are icy cold. They are all linked, so what happens to one ocean affects them all.

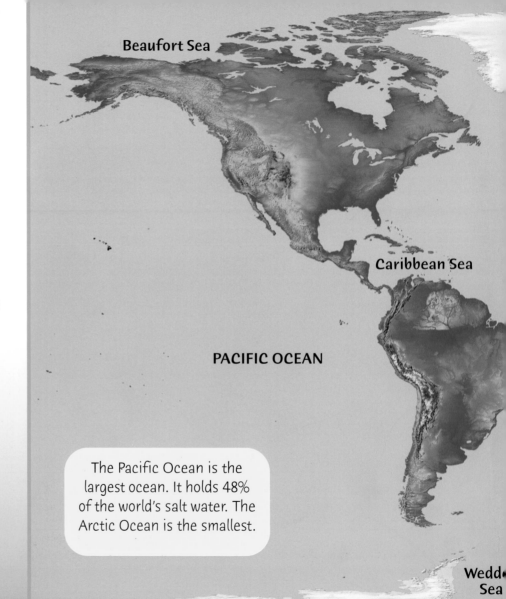

Beaufort Sea

Caribbean Sea

PACIFIC OCEAN

Wedd...
Sea

The Pacific Ocean is the largest ocean. It holds 48% of the world's salt water. The Arctic Ocean is the smallest.

ARCTIC OCEAN

Barents Sea
White Sea

Kara Sea

Bering Sea

North Sea

Baltic
Sea

Caspian
Sea

Black Sea

Aral Sea

Sea of
Okhotsk

Sea of
Japan

Yellow Sea

Mediterranean Sea

East
China
Sea

Red Sea

Arabian
Sea

South
China
Sea

Andaman
Sea

ATLANTIC
OCEAN

INDIAN OCEAN

Arafura Sea

Coral Sea

Tasman
Sea

What is a sea?
A sea is part of the
ocean which has some
land surrounding it.

SOUTHERN OCEAN

5

Oceans in motion

The oceans are never still. Twice a day the tides rise and fall.
Wind pushes the water around, making currents. The energy created by tides
and waves shapes our coastlines by wearing away the rocks and cliffs.

The sea can give life and take life. Some of the most violent storms begin at sea. Hurricanes or cyclones are revolving storms that form over the ocean. They gather heat and energy from warm water, then speed towards the shore.

the centre of the storm

In 2005, Hurricane Katrina hit the city of New Orleans, USA. Huge floods destroyed everything in their path.

Huge ocean waves caused by underwater earthquakes are called tsunami. These can't be seen out in the ocean. They gather speed as they get closer to land, travelling up to 800 kilometres per hour. They can push up a wall of water as high as 40 metres.

On December 26th 2004, an earthquake in the Andaman Sea caused a massive tsunami that killed thousands of people.

Life beneath the waves

For many years what was beneath the sea was a deep mystery. People only knew what they could see above it or what they caught from below it.

In the 1940s Jacques Cousteau invented a piece of equipment called the aqualung, which allowed people to breathe underwater. People could now explore under the sea much more easily and they began to understand more about this unknown place.

Diving with an aqualung is called S.C.U.B.A. diving, which stands for Self-Contained Underwater Breathing Apparatus.

A snorkel is for breathing at the surface.

A face mask helps the diver to see.

An air tank allows the diver to breathe.

A regulator transports air from the tank to the diver.

A vest helps the diver to float.

Gauges show how much air is left.

A weight belt helps the diver to sink.

A wetsuit keeps the diver warm.

Fins make it easy to swim.

Beneath the waves it's a different world. There are many strange and wonderful living things. Some are so small they can't be seen by the human eye. Others are massive, such as the blue whale, the world's largest animal. The ocean's inhabitants can be put in groups.

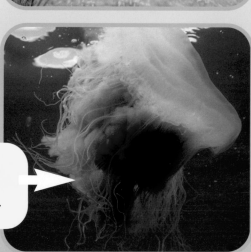

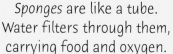

Plants such as seaweed and sea grass cling to rocks. Some plants are so small you need a microscope to see them.

Sponges are like a tube. Water filters through them, carrying food and oxygen.

Coelenterates do not have any bones. This group is made up of jellyfish, corals and sea anemones.

Crustaceans, such as crabs or lobsters, have a hard outer skeleton that they shed each time they grow.

Molluscs have a shell, but some, such as squid and sea slugs, have learnt to live without them.

Echinoderms have spikes and hundreds of tube feet. Sea urchins and starfish belong to this group.

Fish have spines and breathe through **gills**.

Reptiles such as saltwater crocodiles and sea snakes can live on land and in the sea.

Mammals like dolphins and whales live in the sea but breathe air and feed their young with milk.

13

Living together

All living things depend on one another.

| The plants in the sea trap the sun's energy and turn it into food. | → | These plants are eaten by tiny animals called plankton, which are newly hatched shrimps, crabs, fish and sea worms that float with the currents. | → | They are eaten by fish, which are then eaten by bigger fish. |

This is called a food chain.

Not all sea creatures eat each other. Some need each other to survive.

Fish known as "cleaner fish" eat parasites off bigger fish. They get a meal and the big fish gets cleaned.

Sometimes sea creatures share food. The giant grouper eats its food, while the small trevally fish clean up the scraps it leaves behind.

Sometimes one creature uses another for food or transport, such as the remora fish on this manta ray.

Sometimes sea creatures protect each other. Small fish hide in the tentacles of this jellyfish.

16

Strange but true

There are many weird and wonderful animals living in the oceans.

Did you know:

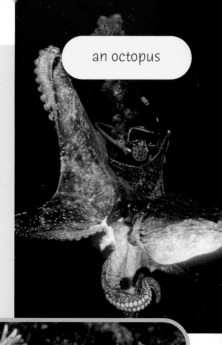
an octopus

★ Octopuses are very intelligent. They can solve mazes and unscrew jar lids to get at the food inside.

★ Giant squid are the largest animal without a backbone in the world. They grow up to 20 metres long and have eyeballs larger than dinner plates.

★ Mantis shrimps have powerful claws that move as fast as a bullet.

★ Starfish break down their food by pouring their stomach out through their mouth then sucking it all back in again.

a mantis shrimp

starfish eating mussels

Living communities

Coral reefs

When plants and creatures live together it's called an ecosystem. Coral reefs are one kind of ecosystem. A coral reef is made by tiny animals called polyps.

Each coral polyp builds a small shell around itself for protection. When the polyp dies its shell is left behind. New polyps grow on top of the shells. Over many years a coral reef is formed.

a polyp

Coral grows one centimetre per year.

Coral reefs are home to many different marine animals. A reef needs sunlight and shallow warm water to survive. If the reef dies so will the animals that live on it.

Hurricanes and storms can destroy reefs but people are the biggest threat.
Already more than a quarter of the Earth's coral reefs have been destroyed by global warming, pollution and fishing.

19

Some reefs are mined. The coral is used for roads and is crushed to make cement. This kills the reef and leaves the coast open to erosion.

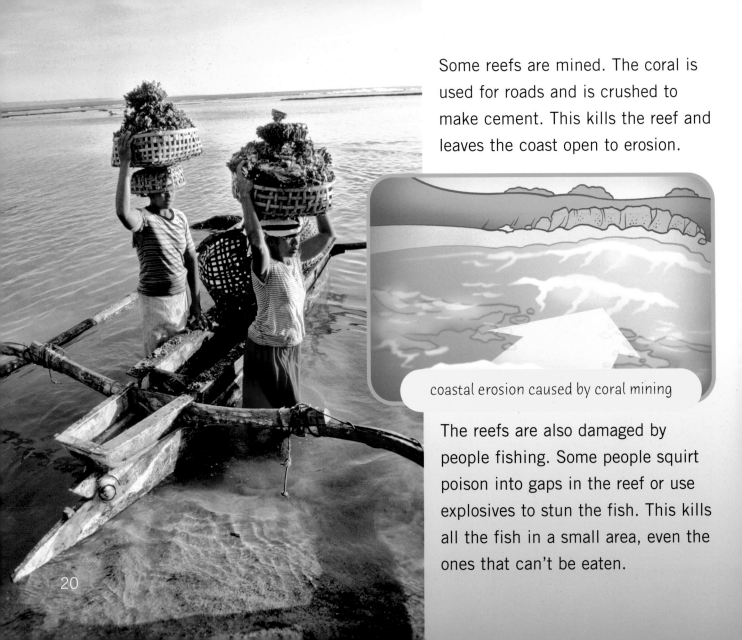

coastal erosion caused by coral mining

The reefs are also damaged by people fishing. Some people squirt poison into gaps in the reef or use explosives to stun the fish. This kills all the fish in a small area, even the ones that can't be eaten.

Coral reefs are beautiful.
Many countries are encouraging
tourists to visit their reefs.
They are making areas into
marine reserves, which are special
places where people can look but
can't fish or touch anything.

Tourists view the reef from a glass-bottom boat.

a sunken boat

Artificial reefs are
being created in
some places by
sinking boats in
areas where coral
can grow on them.

Oceans under threat

Pollution

Pollution comes in many forms: air pollution, sewage, chemicals and land rubbish. Millions of kilograms of rubbish are thrown into the sea every year.

Birds are looking for food amongst rubbish that has been washed ashore.

Old plastic fishing nets and plastic bags kill hundreds of marine animals every year. Turtles and other animals try to eat plastic bags, thinking that they are jellyfish. The bags suffocate them, or get stuck in their stomachs.

rubbish on the coast of Tuvalu

Fish, crabs, birds and seals become entangled in abandoned fishing nets. They are then unable to get food or defend themselves against predators.

A sea lion is caught in a net.

Oil spills

Oil on the ocean is deadly. It floats on the surface, covering everything in its path. Spills occur when oil wells leak, or when ships carrying oil have an accident.

A tanker spills its oil over the ocean.

Cleaning up

Small oil spills a long way from land may be broken up by the waves, or by spraying strong detergents onto them. If the spill is close to land, the chemicals in the detergent might harm marine life, so other solutions must be found.

Straw, peat or polystyrene can be spread on the oil. When the oil has been absorbed, it will be collected.

Floating barriers called "booms" are used to stop the oil, then a tanker sucks the oil off the surface.

Spraying strong detergent onto an oil spill can break it up.

A boom stops the oil spreading.

In 1996 a tanker called the *Sea Empress* ran aground off the coast of south-west Wales and 72,000 tonnes of crude oil leaked into the sea. It took more than a year to clean up the oil spill.

In another spill, little penguins living on the coast of Australia became covered in oil. It clogged their feathers and the penguins couldn't keep warm, so people knitted small woollen jumpers for the penguins. The penguins wore their jumpers until their feathers had been cleaned and they could be returned to the sea.

cleaning up after an oil spill

Overfishing

In the past, people used to catch only enough fish to feed their families. Then they realised they could make money from fishing and boats with huge drift nets began to fish the oceans.

Drift nets are like long curtains which can reach 30 metres deep and 80 kilometres wide. These nets trap everything in their path.

overfishing using a drift net

Purse Seine boats have a net with a huge, wide mouth. The net is towed behind the ship and can catch a whole school of tuna at once. Sometimes dolphins feeding on the tuna become caught in the nets.

Some tuna boats use a long line. These can be 100 kilometres long and have 30,000 hooks attached. Big factory ships collect the fish from the tuna boats so that they can keep fishing for weeks and weeks. This means that the boats catch more fish than are being born each year.

Whales

Some species, like whales, have been hunted until there are almost none left. At first, they were hunted for food. Then it was discovered that many parts of the whale could be used to make different products.

Fuel and grease were made from the blubber. Bones were ground for fertiliser, or used for building materials. Teeth were sold as souvenirs.

29

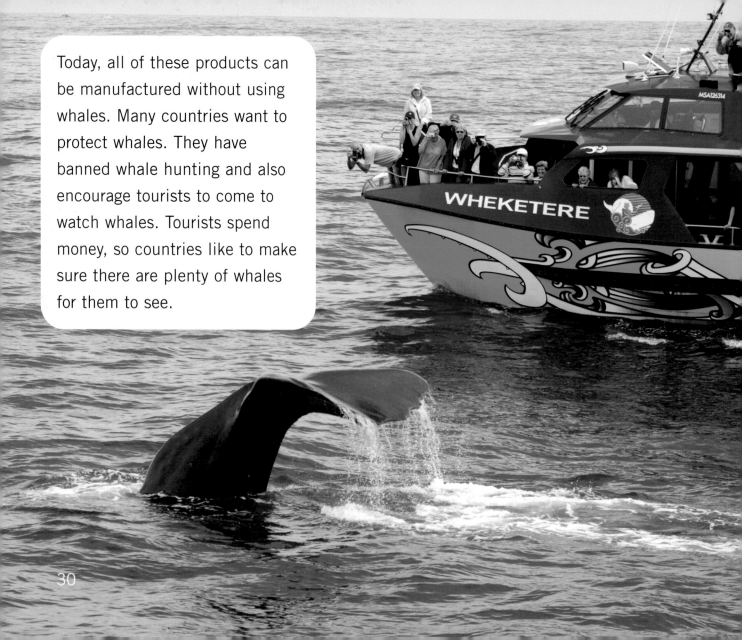

Today, all of these products can be manufactured without using whales. Many countries want to protect whales. They have banned whale hunting and also encourage tourists to come to watch whales. Tourists spend money, so countries like to make sure there are plenty of whales for them to see.

Some whales live in the same area all their lives. Others travel long distances to feeding and breeding grounds. Sometimes they become stranded on beaches. No one knows exactly why this happens.

In 2006 a northern bottle-nosed whale made its way up the River Thames to central London. Rescuers tried to get the whale to turn around and swim back downstream, but it grew weaker and weaker. The whale was put on inflatable pontoons and lifted onto a barge. Unfortunately, it died before the barge reached the ocean.

The stranded whale is put on inflatable pontoons.

Working with the ocean

Dr Ingrid Visser studies Orca or killer whales. If people see an Orca near the coast they phone her. She sails out to watch the whales. Sometimes she puts a hydrophone over the side of the boat so that she can listen to and record the sounds they make. Ingrid also photographs their eye patches and dorsal fins to help identify them. She keeps a record of each sighting and plots the Orcas' travel paths around the coast.

One day, Ingrid received a call about a young male Orca that had become stranded on a beach near her home. It was a whale she already knew, which she'd named Ben.

Ben needed to be kept safe until the tide came in. Someone covered him in a sheet. They poured water over him to keep him cool and dug sand from around his fins. Ingrid stayed with Ben, patting him and talking quietly to him.

A special sling was made with rescue mats and large wooden poles. A crane gently lifted Ben and placed him on inflatable pontoons. When the tide came in the boat towed him out to sea. Ben gave a flick of his tail and swam away. He was safe.

Roger Grace is a marine biologist. He spends his time studying the ocean and the impact of people upon it.

Roger spent a lot of time studying drift netting in the Tasman Sea, between Australia and New Zealand. The drift net boats set their nets at dusk. Later in the night, Roger and his friends would climb aboard a small boat and follow the line of buoys stretching 40 kilometres across the ocean. If the buoys were below the surface Roger knew that something big had been caught in the net. Holding his camera, he would carefully dive into the water.

His job was to photograph the animals that had been caught in the nets. Sometimes the animals were tiny inedible fish. Sometimes they were whales, dolphins and sunfish. If a creature was still alive, Roger and his friends would try to cut it free. This was very dangerous work. The nets could catch anything, even a diver.

Roger's photos were used around the world to help people to see the effects of drift netting. Drift netting has now been banned in the Pacific Ocean and Roger hopes it will be banned in every ocean.

A spearfish is caught in a drift net.

Hooker sea lions

Learning about marine life and understanding their habits has helped to stop some species from becoming extinct. Hooker sea lions live in the islands near the Antarctic. They were hunted for food and their skins and by 1829 only five were left. The last five sea lions were left alone and the population began to increase, but they are still under threat. Many get caught in fishing nets.

Scientists want to understand more about these animals so that they can make sure they survive. To do this they use special equipment. They anaesthetise a female Hooker sea lion and fit a transmitter to her back. The transmitter sends information back to the scientists. It tells them where she is, how deep she dives, how often she dives and how fast she swims. The information is passed to the fishing boats in the hope that they will keep away from the sea lions' feeding grounds.

catching a Hooker sea lion

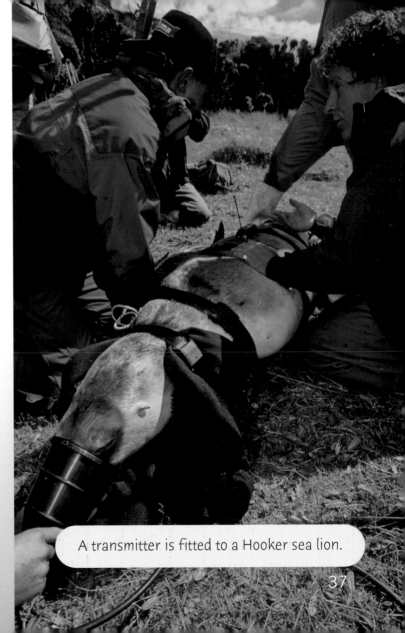

A transmitter is fitted to a Hooker sea lion.

New discoveries

New and exciting discoveries are made in the oceans all the time and some of these can help humans.

Scientists have found a drug made from coral which can help to heal skin tissue that has been badly burned.

Other scientists are studying sponges which may help to cure some types of cancer.

A scientist collects samples of ocean life to study.

The deep ocean is home to many rare species that have never been seen before.

Special underwater submarines and robots collect samples of marine life from these areas to study.

Marine scientists are worried that many of these unknown species will be wiped out. Deep-sea trawlers have nets that can reach down two kilometres and scrape along the seabed, catching thousands of kilograms of fish.

Not all discoveries are in deep water. A new coral reef covering four square kilometres was recently discovered off the coast of Thailand. The reef is full of life. There are species of parrot fish and sweetlips that have never been seen before in these waters.

But how will this new reef be protected? If scuba divers and tourists rush to the reef it could easily be damaged. If people know that there are lots of fish it could become overfished. The exact location of the reef must be kept a secret until a plan is put in place to protect it.

How can we help?

We all need to look after our oceans if they are to stay healthy. Everyone can make a difference.

Here are seven ways we can help:

Reduce

Cut down on the amount of rubbish you make. Don't buy products which have too much packaging, as packaging that has been thrown into the sea kills marine life.

Reuse

A plastic shopping bag can be used as a bin liner. Ice-cream containers make good storage boxes.

Recycle

If you can't reuse something then recycle it.

Learn about the oceans

The more we learn about the oceans, the more we will want to look after them. Join a marine studies group or learn how to snorkel.

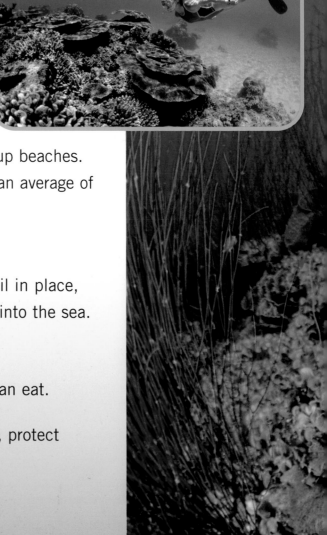

Beach clean-ups

Each year, thousands of volunteers help to clean up beaches. In a recent clean-up in the UK, volunteers found an average of one piece of litter every 52 centimetres.

Plant trees

Trees help to keep our air fresh. They hold the soil in place, so that loose soil doesn't fill our rivers and wash into the sea.

Limit your catch

If you go fishing, don't take more fish than you can eat.

For our oceans to survive we must preserve them, protect them and prevent further pollution.

43

Glossary

anaesthetise — give drugs to take away pain

artificial — made by human beings rather than happening naturally

blubber — the fat of a sea mammal

buoys — floats that are fixed in one place at sea

cargo — goods carried on a ship, aircraft or lorry

detergents — strong chemicals that clean

dorsal — on the upper side or back of an animal or plant

gills — body parts of fish and some reptiles that extract the oxygen from water

hydrophone — a microphone that hears sounds underwater

inedible — can't be eaten

inflatable pontoons — flat-bottom boats blown up with air

manufactured — made by human beings

marine — to do with, or from, the sea

predators — animals that hunt other animals

ran aground — came ashore at the wrong place

school — a group of fish

sewage — waste product from human beings

transmitter — equipment that transmits radio signals

Index

aqualung   9, 10

Arctic Ocean   4, 5

Atlantic Ocean   4, 5,

coral   11, 18–21, 38, 40

cyclones   7

dolphins   13, 28, 34

global warming   19

hurricanes   7, 19

Indian Ocean   4, 5

jellyfish   16, 22

octopuses   17

oil spills   24–26

Orca   32

overfishing   27

Pacific Ocean   4, 35

penguins   26

plankton   14

plants   11, 14, 18

pollution   19, 22

polyps   18

S.C.U.B.A. diving   10

sea lions   23, 36, 37

shrimps   14, 17

squid   12, 17

Southern Ocean   4, 5

starfish   12, 17

tsunami   8

tuna   28

whales   11, 13, 29–31, 34

Save our oceans!

Our oceans are in danger from:

- overfishing
- drift netting
- oil spills
- pollution

If we don't do something now, some sea creatures may become extinct!